DISCARD

*Gift of
Paul Marion
2018*

The Gardener and the Bees
Helena Minton

Pollard Memorial Library
401 Merrimack Street
Lowell, MA 01852

Copyright © 2006
Helena Minton
March Street Press
3413 Wilshire
Greensboro NC 27408
marchstreetpress.com
rbixby@earthlink.net
isbn 1-59661-056-5

Table of Contents

I
Perennial Bed ≈ 3
Standing at the Trellis Before Supper ≈ 4
Turnip ≈ 5
Crows in the Cul-de-Sac ≈ 7
Mulch ≈ 9
In Pittsburg, New Hampshire ≈ 10
Day Surgery Pre-Op ≈ 12
The Wasp Nest in My Neighbor's Magnolia ≈ 13
Peonies ≈ 14
Building the Compost ≈ 16
Gerbera Daisy ≈ 18

II
January ≈ 23
Coda ≈ 24
The Birch ≈ 26
Wedding Day ≈ 27
Scrutiny ≈ 28
The Distance Garden ≈ 29
At the Marie Selby Botanical Gardens ≈ 31
The Manatee Tank ≈ 33
At the Feeder ≈ 35
Convalescence Among Blueberries ≈ 36
Crabapple ≈ 37
Tasks ≈ 38

Grateful acknowledgment is made to the following publications where some of these poems first appeared, sometimes in different form: *The Bridge* (online), *The Larcom Review, The Merrimack Literary Review, The Mystic River Review* (online), *Red River Review* (online), *Renovation, Sou'wester, Sojourner, Solo, West Branch.*

I would like to thank the members of my writing group for helping me shape these poems: Kathleen Aguero, Suzanne Berger, Erica Funkhouser, Celia Gilbert, Miriam Goodman, Nina Nyhart, and Cornelia Veenendaal.

I would also like to thank Tara Masih for her editing assistance.

These poems are dedicated to the memory of
my father, Robert William Minton, 1918–2000.

Perennial Bed

In September the bees spend hours
on the saucers of rose sedum,
their curled legs moving over petals
fleshy as rubber brushes.
I thought bees never stood still.
These hardly move,
becoming both the needle
and the painstaking fingers that hold them
until they cover each inch of tapestry.

This one lands on a filament
of coreopsis moonbeam,
floating down, down to the dirt,
then flung back
through the undulating architecture.
Righting itself, it begins to investigate
the intricate netting, old bridal veil,
tiny yellow-tipped buds,
the ignored world at ankle level.

Down on my knees
I toil beside him and the others I see
hidden in the system of green stems.
I hum along, drawn in
by their noisy concentration.
Nothing gets in their way,
not my elbow, my shadow, my scent.
Let them sting me,
brash as I am.

Standing at the Trellis
Before Supper

It's always better to let someone
underestimate you.

Did the string bean say that?
Friend I didn't know I had,
staple of my great-grandparents'
farm in Foremost, Alberta.

Diligence. Industry.
Only now do I understand
how they buckled down,
nose to grindstone.

Blue Lake, Kentucky Wonder,
subtle but abundant
among its dusty vines, a military green,
now-you-see-it-now-you-don't,
like the brown egg that blends into the straw.

A cherry tomato named
Camp Joy, garden bauble,
shines pearl and silver green
as it ripens, tempting radiance,

but the bean hangs where it's always hung,
the garden's understatement,
unassuming, but vertical,
practical, plumb, a fact
like the pencil line I was taught
sails on into infinity.

Turnip

The clerk who weighs it doesn't know its name.
Her ancestors, like mine,

must have dug one up, good-sized,
like a baby's head

grateful for turnip
instead of stones.

I carry one home
to pare for the holiday meal,

to chip at waxy skin that falls,
not smooth and seamless

as apple peel but in small flakes
before I slice and drop

the orange chunks in boiling water.
On each plate I place a spoonful

to ward off hunger,
put dirt back under our fingernails,

our hands back in the dirt
around the vegetable that grows

in war, when soldiers raid abandoned farms,
dig up gardens with their bayonets,

and resisters, hidden in root cellars,
hear footsteps above them,

chairs being smashed for firewood
as they tear at the skin with their teeth.

Crows in the Cul-de-Sac

The backyard's basic black
lives at the edge of things, like the deer,
not one to fly into deep wood
in search of caves and vanish.

He likes a mown lawn,
chrysanthemum seeds, my garbage,
happy with what we human beings
have done to North America,

staying close to a house
as he pecks, the way a child plays
by himself while adults talk,
a child who learns to count
by counting crows.

The crow is my slip showing,
a run in my stocking,
late for the bus.

Two crows are sisters
who talk every day on the phone,
irritate each other across the wire
but don't hang up, discuss the little
details of their lives
no one else cares about.

Three crows conspire
near my neighbor's oak tree.

This is also my crow:
thumbprint on white paper,
shadow no one mentions,

a spot on the X-ray
the doctor says is nothing serious,
he'll just keep an eye on it,
a bird's eye.

Four crows figure
in proposition bets;
which one will fly off the fence first?

More than five crows gather
on the grassy oval
and I'm tempted to pull the shade
but I turn my head
and there's only one again,
my crow, my condition,
in the maple, the bare lilac branches.

Mulch

Grass littered with torn leaves
I sprinkled in the flowerbeds
to smother weeds
has dried to straw,

a gray that persuades me
human hair keeps growing
in the grave.

The ground gives back
what I least want to see.
My efforts cry ugly.

Mulch frightens me,
decaying matter,
not smoothed-over
like my neighbors' lawns,
edged an even green,
neat as hospital corners.

I'm reminded
mulch is a matter of madness,
of a woman tearing her hair.

The one who started
as everyone's darling
is now on her knees
in a corner, rocking,

not quite out of sight,
as I claw at this year's blossoms.

In Pittsburg, New Hampshire

I liked the fact that he knew
where he was going.

He strolled down a driveway,
turned right on the dirt road,
walked straight a stone's throw
and took a left toward Glen Lodge
like a postman on his daily route.

I had to tell someone what I'd witnessed.
To my listener, a young man by the lake,
my hands described
the male's tea-colored antlers.
A *bull*, he mildly corrected,
dropping his bucket in the water.
Haven't seen a bull around in a while.

A local pastime near the Quebec border:
to motor slowly at dusk along the bogs and swamps,
the curve of the Connecticut Lakes.
Searchlights attached to their car windows,
drivers and passengers scrutinize
darkening limbs and leaves.
To the novice, every shadow
announces the full animal,
each branch holds an antler's arabesque.

It was morning. I was on foot, alone,
in the silent, still-green September,
sun filtering down, no wind,
glad to encounter him and relieved
he turned away without seeing me.

I've heard people go their whole lives
without seeing a moose.

To have seen him vanish—
unable to ever call him back,
to have watched the nonchalance
of disappearing hooves, hindquarters,
tail and bony rack—
each antler tip with its own name—
brow, bay, royal, and *surroyal.*

Day Surgery Pre-Op

Only two of us today:
me and a young man from a halfway house
who rubs his hands and whispers to himself;
on his lap a hairbrush and a Bible.
Will someone meet him after?

I feel a tenderness toward him,
my friend in fear.
What if we don't wake up?

Other fears,
of heights, of flying,
are holidays compared to this.

That's why we're startled
Monday morning
by surgery doors opening,
wide as supermarket doors,
as young surgeons
and nurses in blue scrubs
enter chatting and laughing.

For a moment I remember
waking in the dark to hear my parents
call good night to friends,
their voices loosed on the street,
and closing my eyes,
happy things went on while I slept.

The Wasp Nest
in My Neighbor's Magnolia

The nest wintered above my head
in the gray branches
I walk past each morning.
I'd like to knock it out of the tree with a stick.

The magnolia blooms
pink and white like a girl
in her *quinceañera* dress.
The nest rests like a *piñata*
before it's decorated,
a basket of ash, a head,
light as death, half-hidden
by the petals' waxy bloat.

I feel I know the dark interior hollow,
could lower it over my hair
and walk, an eyeless monster.
A disturbance across my mind
from time to time,
it isn't hurting anyone, any more
than a twig in the road.

Yet I don't forget this force
of nature a few feet from my house
a swarm spun with furious methodical industry.
It prods my urge to covet or destroy.
I will it to disintegrate
layer by papery layer.
I'd like to grab my neighbor's arm and ask,
What is it still doing here?

Peonies

Rain has beaten the peonies.
They were standing tall yesterday,
top-heavy, guy-wired, half open in their hoops.

Now they spill on the asphalt,
stems bent, dragged down by their heads,
edges soiled,
exploded and scattered
beside the slender
controlled rose.

Petals litter the ground
like the morning after a gala—
someone has to clean up.

Peonies live large,
showy and glowing,
big guns of the suburbs.

They should not have been planted
on a slant beside the driveway
but I won't move them now.
I have done what I have to
to keep them alive.

Cupping a bloom in my hands
I feel a pulse
as in a bird's body.

The Gardener and the Bees

I've read that peonies thrive
for generations on old farms,
rain washing the soil down
from the cow pasture
to the gardens by the house.

As I walk from my car
I have only to brush against them
and they fall apart.

Building the Compost

They talk about it for a year.

She wants to throw the rinds
behind the woodshed.

He says they need a frame
wrapped with chicken wire.

All summer she urges him to build
not sure why she's so desperate.

Try it yourself, he says.

She walks to the workbench,
touches the tools,
tears falling in the sawdust.

After the first frost
he builds a frame
as big as a walk-in closet.

It reminds her of the cage
where the witch locked Hansel
though she only imagines the bars.

It might be a fort,
a cupola where she can play with dolls,
a space to stand when she is angry.

The Gardener and the Bees

It is her turn.
She hammers horseshoe tacks
against the chicken wire.

Now, he thinks, she will be happy.

She finds herself moving
toward the thrift
of a woman in wartime,
saving scraps, starting seeds
for a victory garden.

Gerbera Daisy

How had I missed it?
I was well in middle age
before I noticed
the oval color-fast petals.

At her sister's wedding
my cousin, maid-of-honor,
held, not baby's breath,
but a clutch of orange Gerberas

against her dark green velvet sheath,
so bold a gesture, so impertinent
in the unadorned
9th-century stone chapel,

coming out of nowhere,
surprising as the wooden flutes
the Andean musicians played
on the lawn of the estate.

I saw that this was not a field flower
picked while the mind was elsewhere.
It traveled on a leafless stalk,
thick and straight

as if it could survive without water.
At the bloom's center,
like a schoolgirl's prize,
the round sponge: gold or black.

The Gardener and the Bees

I hadn't been to England in thirty years
or seen the girls since they were children.
I kept them as little faces
in the meadow in the photograph.

How tall the girls were now
posing on the terrace of the great house.
Civil War re-enactors had rented
the grounds for the weekend.

Rifles at their sides,
they lined the gravel drive
in salute to the wedding party.
I wandered off, away from the reception.

An antique motorcycle museum
was housed in an old garage
at the edge of a walled garden,
the mortar crumbling

among wild roses, a covey of them,
their disintegrating petals
opened to whitish interiors.
Roses, I recognized.

Their long vines gave my hands an itch
to find a pair of pruning shears
and trim the ramblers
caught along the gate.

Admit it: the world
had risen up around me
determined in its preferences,
overgrown as weeds through stone.

January

You left in the gray beginnings.

Animals slept underfoot.
Kings walked into the barn
two weeks late with gifts

and nothing could make it warm
not my will or lists
of ways I would be better.

Time not to ask too much
of myself or others
but to bend to work at hand

the paths I had to shovel
and to walk along stone walls
snow covered

but I knew were there.

Coda

You used to say it ran in families
this sense of time.
Your wristwatch glinting
beneath a crisp cuff
you set the standard
but it wasn't a strictness
you instilled, more of a personal attribute
like the way we smile
or move our hands when we talk.
It makes us feel better to be on time.

From the moment I heard you were sick
and I flew south
I fell behind.
When I arrived
they were already sweeping
your hospital room
preparing your bed
for someone else.

I thought I'd be at loose ends
yet even months later I feel
I will never catch up.
What I'm racing toward
is not the ocean liner
pulling away in a dream
but minutiae,
chores and purchases,
three calendars I mark
and forget to double-check,
bills, letters, phone calls.

Why is it so satisfying
to cross out *milk*
or *dry cleaning*,
to gun my way
to the next errand?

I've forgotten what it's like
not to know what to do next.
Grief has become a bureaucracy.
I go through channels
to reach you.
I clutch my lists in line,
thinking of you,
your congeniality, your wit,
your traits become
small things written down.

The Birch

The week before my wedding
how did we find a moment,
my father and I, who rarely
worked together with our hands?
During the tissue-paper preparations
it felt urgent that we dig,
heft the compact root ball,
lower it, pack in the dirt.
Less urgent as we stood back
and admired what we'd planted,
white trunk with fringed leaves,
a head taller than the ring bearer.
Underfoot, myrtle spread
its intangible blue flowers.

Wedding Day

Out of the branches, inch-long bodies fell
all afternoon, softly, on the patio,
on the chairs and the tablecloths
as the brown creatures stripped trees of green.
My father paid the grandchildren
a penny a bug to collect them.
The caterpillars don't appear in any pictures.
They never dropped in my hair
or landed on the neck of a guest,
or were caught in David's Mexican wedding shirt.
I like to think they slept through the ceremony,
stopped their work out of respect,
like gravediggers who lean on their shovels
to watch a wedding party pass.
They were there in the darkness of mid-June,
chewing through the reception, the music,
hardly a plague or an omen,
but a suburb's pestilence,
an arborist's headache,
part of family lore, part of the story,
cobwebby, their fur pettable,
the children not frightened
as they filled their buckets,
the insects' gauzy white tents
strung between the maples' limbs,
close to lovely from this distance.

Scrutiny

Years ago she was asked
to record her favorites
in the form of nouns:
blue, avocado, silk.
Now her list is private,
365 things to do:
hang the hummingbird feeder,
try to grow allium again,
make jello salad.
No one scrutinizes her desires.
The binoculars trained downstream,
she's left to fill in her own blanks
with a steady heartbeat.
At the old armory, de-toothed
and put to new uses,
the bricks' right angles
assure her a place for her thoughts
like a doll cupboard
with 20 tiny drawers.
She asks nothing more
than to follow the signs
to the Commodore's House:
366th on her list.
Around the corner from the limelight:
her extended hyphenate of endeavors.

The Distance Garden

Shiver of stems before blooming,
sun thrown on grass,
I look for the romantic
in a suburban yard
and wonder if yearning
is inherited
like a long waist
or blue eyes
or a taste for cantaloupe.

My mother turned
years ago, as we passed a house,
to murmur *lilacs.*
The word carried the weight
of more than a shrub.
It held whole flowerbeds.
When I looked back
we were passing another yard,
with its own bend in the branches.

An inviting shadow
scattered on the lawn
reminded her of an acre
in her childhood
at the prairie's edge.
Why did it have to be so far away?

Each time I start a garden
I think of the borders

she grew up walking in.
Their corners come back to me
in moments like dry leaves
blown against a fence
where a slender vine
begins its climb.

The Marie Selby Botanical Gardens

I stroll past hibiscus,
jacaranda and frangipani,
through the black shadows of the banyan,
crushed oyster shells underfoot,
in the early morning Florida cold
sharp as a comb across the scalp.

I am trying, as I tried last year,
to learn the difference
between palmate and pinnate,
royal and sabal,
and the lower fanned shrubs
which look like palms but are not.

In this chill oranges must be protected.
I blow on my fingertips.
My earlobes ache.
I imagine the shock of the orchid
lifted from a Borneo cliff,
carried here by hand
to be tended and displayed.

Bending my head in this botanical cold
is my discipline,
a kind my mother knew
walking to school
through Saskatchewan snowdrifts.
Who said we should suffer
to study flowers?

Out in the open a moment,
I feel the sun's deep compress
on my neck, like a brand,
a coin of faith, of gratitude.

By noon the air has evened out
to its famous softness.
My skin takes for granted
hovering wings,
even shadows have warmed,
and the soil,
like heated petals to my touch.

The Manatee Tank

Romaine lettuce heads float on the top of the tank,
every inch covered with leaves.
The tank is a study in green: green white
of the belly undersides, the lacy edge of leaves,
Sarasota sunlight spiraling down,
offering lime, moss, forest, and sea
and the darker spruce shadows I stand in.

I wonder if manatee like the hearts,
and how many heads a day they eat,
preferring iceberg,
though romaine is more nutritious.
I've also leaned at the kitchen counter,
tearing off leaves, mindlessly chewing.
That must be what we have in common,
a shared love of salad
and the talent to pass hours
nibbling, adrift.

The teenage girls who crowd the glass beside me
squeal that these thousand-pound mammals
brushing past the glass are trying to kiss them.
The girls want to kiss back,
or climb in and stroke the slippery sides
of Hugh and Buffet, of the order Sirenia,
pat the pink heads and flippers, tails an afterthought.

I imagine the girls also have the know-how
to idle away an afternoon,

lying on pillows across the living room floor,
brushing their hair, the strands
rising up in the light as if it were water,
while their mothers, who shoo them out, to accomplish,
not to waste the best part of the day,
to breathe fresh air, may have forgotten
the desire to be suspended safely in bodies
so odd they endear themselves to the world.

At the Feeder

The sound of running water
draws the hummingbird she says
as she stirs the sugar water,
fills the feeder by the fuchsia near the kitchen
where she stands at the sink,
her day organized
around the bird's arrival.

A minute shift in light
signals he's there,
blur of a blur, suspended
on the other side of the screen
a few inches from her face,
her companion shadow.

What can I call her? Resigned...Stoic?
Patience makes her at home
in the care she shows
rinsing a dish, her feet
steady on clean linoleum

drawing strength from
the way she was raised:
to be frugal,
to attend to detail:
the correction, the counter-shift
at the window
as he whirs away.

Convalescence Among Blueberries

Butter, sugar, and eggs
wait on the counter
below a watercolor
I bought for you last week:
blueberries balanced on a branch,
like a delicate detail
of a Japanese screen.

In the yard, one arm in a sling,
you instruct me
in the art of the harvest.
I learn what to look for
among the fluted leaves,
the darker, the sweeter the blue.

Guarded by two sharp-shinned hawks
that keep the sparrows thin,
berries roll off our thumbs
into the colander.
The pint shines, brimful,
in late summer's royal pail.

Crabapple

In a plan to pare
I stared out the window:
how to make it round
like the trees on the hillside orchard.

In bed, anticipating
the outcome, the satisfaction
of the hauling away,
I felt the oiled shears in my hands,
the way I would wield them so vividly,
it might have been a dream at night
in which an entire act
is carried out to completion.

On that morning I turned
to lead limbs
outlined among gray clouds,
entered a hazy tunnel,
unable to follow a branch
in toward the trunk
or out to the tips
without getting lost.

My shears struck
resistant wood.
Each silvery twist
had a twin,
as though the severed shoots
kept growing back.
I still wait for instruction
from the patient
weight-bearing tree.

Tasks

I grow to respect shade
and the cool it proffers;
the Japanese rhododendron,
its leaves the dark brown of expensive leather;
and the yellow tuberous begonia
waiting like a cat underfoot.

Hosta seems too fleshy,
its methodical leaves
spread along the driveway
to mute the edge,
but to love hosta
is like a Buddhist call
to embrace what is at hand.

I am learning to enter a garden
without judgment, eyes open
but benign, alert to the rustle
of autumn grass,

the idea that a border must be beautiful
like a table set for guests,
relinquished,
to know a garden
as a kind of abstraction,
a way into difficulty.

The Gardener and the Bees

The plots of dirt are laboratories
in which to experiment;
chess with sun and shadow,
my move: bee balm
to the open where it belongs.

Deeper into the green
my hands delve.
They no longer trace defeat
in this mirror of earth.